The Science of Living

Proverbs: Ancient and Modern

Adages with Explanations

Enrique Fiesta

Mendon Cottage Books

Mendon Cottage Books

JD-Biz Publishing

Disclaimer

The information is this book is provided for informational purposes only. It is not intended to be used and medical advice or a substitute for proper medical treatment by a qualified health care provider. The information is believed to be accurate as presented based on research by the author.

The contents have not been evaluated by the U.S. Food and Drug Administration or any other Government or Health Organization and the contents in this book are not to be used to treat cure or prevent disease.

The author or publisher is not responsible for the use or safety of any diet, procedure or treatment mentioned in this book. The author or publisher is not responsible for errors or omissions that may exist.

Warning

The Book is for informational purposes only and before taking on any diet, treatment or medical procedure, it is recommended to consult with your primary health care provider.

Our books are available at

1. Amazon.com
2. Barnes and Noble
3. Itunes
4. Kobo
5. Smashwords
6. Google Play Books

Table of Contents

Introduction

I find that one of the ways to cut through the complexity of everyday life and simplify my experience of things is to rely upon the wisdom of our ancestors. Adages are one the greatest ways to do this, because they are the distilled wisdom of over 60,000 years of human history.

They are often incisive, direct, and to the point. If we apply them earnestly to our own life situations we will often find that their wisdom flies far higher than our own ideas and contrivances.

The adage, unfortunately, has lost its prestige in the modern era for a number of reasons, but probably the most significant one is that modern readers do not like to be lectured nor preached to. An adage, unlike an analytic argument or witty retort, acquires its force not from the ingenuity of an individual but from its historicity and ancient pedigree. In this regard, an adage is similar to a Bible verse. Many secular persons despise having the Bible quoted at length to support an argument against them since they do not believe in, trust, nor particularly care for the ancient wisdom of the Bible- they generally share the same disdain for ancient adages since they are often rooted in the genius of a race of people rather than in a clever person's ability to churn out witty statements.

Adages also carry with them a moralistic tone which censures unreasonable, bad, and slothful behavior. Modern man, with his obsequious desire for licentiousness and indifference, tends to reject wisdom and knowledge which he is unable to access with his meager powers. Autonomy is prized as the chief good in modern society. Unfortunately, autonomy and licentiousness are not the chief goods of existence-rather, existence itself is prior in the order of importance since autonomy and license could not exist without existing first. It is the nature of existence that we must study if we are to discover true happiness. Modern man's worship of autonomy will only, in the end, leave him grasping for answers and truths in a chaotic world.

Adages with Explanations

Stupid is as stupid does.

An adage made famous from the movie *Forrest Gump*. This particular proverb is used to express the idea that you tell a person's intelligence based upon their actions. If someone consistently does stupid things, one must necessarily conclude that he is stupid. The proverb works conversely as well, as an intelligent person will consistently act intelligently.

Your mother is always right.

An expression which encapsulates the idea that your maternal parent possesses wisdom surpassing your own when it comes to decision making. The adage likely has its origins in the fact that mothers often know their children better than they know themselves.

Between friends all is common.

A modern equivalent is "mi casa is su casa" (Spanish for "my house is your house"). This expression embodies the sentiment that true friends are supposed to share everything between themselves. On an even deeper level, it can mean that true friends share common virtues, beliefs, and habits. Related to the idea that "birds of a feather, flock together" as friends of a common character, are friends together.

Trouble experienced makes a fool wise.

One of the problems with the inexperienced is that they lack wisdom. Oftentimes, we become wiser when we encounter troubles and realize that the cause of the trouble was due to our inexperience. Aristotle, the Greek philosopher, noted that the best way to acquire wisdom is to be taught but that the most common way, and the most painful, is through experience.

The unexpected appearance of a God.

This proverb is most usually seen in its Latin form "*Deus ex machine.*" The proverb is applied to oftentimes contentious, difficult, or terrible circumstances which are alleviated by the sudden and unexpected appearance of someone or something which resolves the issues without significant difficulties. For instance, in the movie *Alien* the character Ripley attempts to kill the titular monster by self-destructing her spaceship. The sudden appearance of a self-destruct apparatus is a common element in many, many movies.

The ring of Gyges.

The ring of Gyges was mentioned in Plato's *Republic* during a discussion concerning what someone would do if it were impossible for him to be held accountable for his crimes. The ring of Gyges granted the wearer invisibility which made it possible for him to do whatever he wanted without impunity. The adage is related to the notion that "absolute power corrupts absolutely," as one with absolute power can do whatever he wills without punishment.

To drive out one nail by another.

This is used to describe situations wherein someone attempts to drive away trouble with the same trouble. A similar modern expression is "to fight fire with fire." It is also used to describe a situation where one drives away trouble with a similar trouble.

The sword of Damocles.

The sword of Damocles is a classical allusion where a king's (named Damocles) obsequious servant praised what he perceived to be the high quality of life the king led. The king, hearing this, asked the servant if he wished to live his life. The servant said yes. The king ordered that the servant be sat in a golden throne in front of a table laden with a lavish abundance of fine food; however, he also ordered that a sword be tied to the ceiling by a single strand of horse hair above the head of the servant. The servant, fearing for his life, cried out that he did not desire to live the life of the king. The moral of the story is that the king lives only a superficially pleasing life; in fact, he is in constant danger. It is a story showing the moral that we ought not to covet the lives of our betters.

The ancient rhetor and statesman Cicero interpreted the story to be concerning the life of a tyrant. Cicero believed that the tyrant, though he live an opulent life, is actually not happy because he is in constant danger of death.

Nothing good happens after eight.

The expression gives voice to the notion that nothing good occurs at unreasonable times during the night. The time is arbitrary, ranging generally from eight to twelve at night (the time was 2 a.m. in the sitcom *How I Met Your Mother*). There is a resemblance to the biblical idea of the powers of darkness as agents of evil seek to hide their plots from the light (or public); for instance, crimes are typically committed at night so that they can avoid detection.

Those who exalt themselves will be humbled, and those who humble themselves will be exalted.

Biblical wisdom, it has been contemplated and interpreted by hundreds, if not thousands, of years of Christian philosophers and mystics. Medieval schoolmen interpreted the phrase to mean that man had to conform his behavior according to right reason. If man were to conform his behavior according to the dictates of reason and supernatural revelation, he would be in harmony with the balance of the cosmos for man must know his place within God's universe. Therefore he who exalts himself is acting according to unreason and pride and sets himself above God- he will soon be humbled (punitively) by God.

Like rejoices in like.

This phrase refers to the fact that men of common attributes and interests tend to favor and desire the company of one another. The adage may have acquired its force from nature wherein every animal tends to associate intimately with species of its own kind.

Birds of a feather flock together.

Persons of a similar character tend to "flock together" just as birds of the same species flock together. Thus, if one were looking for good people one would find the groups of good men. Criminals and policemen do not associate with one another, but criminals associate with criminals and policemen with policemen.

Well begun is half done.

This adage expresses the idea that merely beginning to work on a task is a substantial step toward completing the task. One of the problems many have with completing tasks is that they never even begin the task. It is an attack on procrastination as well which etymologically means "to put off for tomorrow."

So many men, so many opinions.

Refers to the issue, so many of us encounter, that every single person has an opinion about every single possible issue- from politics to health foods to religious questions. The quotation comes from the Roman comedian Terence. It can be interpreted as an appeal for humility in matters one knows little about. I find conversations tedious where people speak concerning matters they know little about. It is also an appeal to us, as rational beings, to have informed opinions and open minds- we like "so many men" have "many opinions"- what separates our opinions from theirs?

To leave no stone unturned.

An ancient proverbial imperative expressing the notion that every possible effort was spent in the accomplishing of some task.

A small fire is soon quenched.

An ancient Chinese proverb expressing the idea that it is better to deal with problems when they are small than when they are large. It often happens that a fire cannot be quenched if it grows too large; troubles in our own lives are analogous.

You are counting the waves.

Used to indicate that one is engaged in a pointless or infeasible enterprise. It is impossible to count the waves of the ocean, since they never cease- we should not waste our times engaged in useless or futile pursuits.

You write in water.

Another adage expressing the idea that we ought not to engage ourselves in impossible endeavors.

You are building on the sand.

This adage is similar to the preceding two in that building on the sand is not worthwhile or generally feasible. However, it can also be used to express the idea that it is not worthwhile to begin a project without the appropriate preparations. Just as we ought not to teach advanced physics to younglings, we should not build on the sand. If the foundation is inadequate, the structure will not stand.

Between Charybdis and Scylla.

An ancient adage indicating situations wherein all alternative courses of action incur serious disadvantages or hardships. It is an allusion to the *Odyssey* by the Greek epic poet Homer where the hero Odysseus must steer his ship between two different monsters; Charybdis, if encountered, would destroy the ship and all the men whereas Scylla would only kill six men.

The adage can also be an injunction that we act moderately in order to pursue the "golden mean" and avoid excesses and deficiencies of virtues. It applies here because Odysseus had to steer between two vices (excess and deficiency) in order to remain safe.

Between a rock and a hard place.

Used to express the idea that all alternatives have difficulties in a particular situation.

The fox knows many things, but the hedgehog knows one big thing.

Although the fox is a clever animal and knows many tricks, it is incapable of overcoming the one big trick of the hedgehog which is to curl into a ball of sharp spikes. The wisdom of this adage is that it prompts us to realize that being multi-talented is not always advantageous. Especially, when one trick is all it takes.

I hold the wolf by the ears.

An admonishment that one's conduct is extremely dangerous. A similar modern expression is to "hold the tiger by the tail."

To be afraid of one's own shadow.

Used to refer to people who fear excessively. An admonishment that we ought not to worry about things which we cannot harm us, or which we cannot change (we cannot remove our shadows).

God helps those who help themselves.

Used to praise the virtues of self-initiative and motivation. It goes hand in hand with the notion that those who persistently use their talents to aid themselves will ultimately be successful.

Know thyself.

A Greek inscription found on the entrance into the Temple of Delphi. There has been thousands of years of interpretation into the meaning of this enigmatic phrase, but it seems to me to express the idea that there can be no wisdom or prudent action on the part of a man if he does not know himself- his character, his beliefs, his desires, etc. If a man does not know he is a coward, and enlists in the military he has done an unwise thing. It is important that one know one's character, otherwise one will make serious mistakes in life.

Wine speaks the truth.

Expresses the well-known fact that people tend to speak more freely under the influence of alcohol.

Man is but a bubble.

An Anglo-Saxon equivalent is that man's life is like a sparrow. Both express the age old wisdom that man's life is very brief. A bubble exists for a short time before popping and disappearing.

One swallow does not make summer.

Warns against presumptuous assertions. Swallows are typically seen in the summer, but just because one sees one it does not mean summer has begun. The same applies for life situations- just because you see something, it does not necessarily mean that something else has happened despite the fact that it typically does.

Extreme right is extreme wrong.

Another adage praising the life of moderation and an admonishment against extremes of behavior.

For bums it is always a holiday.

Bums do not work, so it always seems like they are on holiday.

Herculean labors.

Refers to a task which requires considerable talents, efforts, and strength (physical or otherwise) to accomplish. The adage arises from the myth of Hercules. In order for Hercules to atone for his crimes, he was ordered to complete twelve labors for the king Eurystheus. The twelve labors included in order: slaying the Nemean lion, Lernaean hydra, Eurymanthian boar, Ceryneian hind, Stymphalian birds, retrieving the girdle of Hippolyta, cleaning the Augean stables, steal the Cretan bull, and taming the mares of Diomedes. In addition he had to fetch apples from the Hesperides and capture the Cerberus because he did not complete two the 12 labors solely by himself.

Clothes make the man.

Expresses the idea that a man's clothes cause others to view him either lightly or seriously. Mark Twain once commented that no one listens to a naked person. Contrasts with the meaning of "do not judge a book by its cover."

Do not judge a book by its cover.

The appearance of someone or something does not necessarily mean that the inside is just as beautiful or ugly. Compare with "beauty is only surface deep." Jesus Christ appeared to man as a humble, lowly craftsman, but was also God. The Pharisees made the mistake of judging Jesus by his lowly appearance.

Everyone thinks his own fart smells sweet.

A humorous adage dating from the Greeks which refers to the fact that people tend to find their own preferences, attitudes, quirks, and eccentricities as superior to those of others. Compare with "as there are men, there are so many opinions."

The blind leading the blind.

Emerging the Greeks and even the New Testament, the adage warns against following ignorant leaders and points out that the ignorant are often led by ignorant leaders.

War is sweet for those who have not tried it.

Expresses the idea that persons who advocate for war are generally those who have had no experience of fighting in wars, being victims of wars, or experiencing the effects of wars. The great humanist Erasmus wrote a defense of pacifism in relation to this adage.

Custom is a second nature.

Customs are essentially habits. Habits can either be good or bad, but they often make up a great part of our mental dispositions and response to every situation. It is important than that we pursue and instill within ourselves good habits, since they primarily comprise the variety of our actions.

Nothing is sweeter than to know everything.

Similar to the expression "knowledge is power." To know everything is to know the nature of things. All one would have to do is act according to one's knowledge to live a perfect life. Thus, to have knowledge is to have a kind of power over reality.

Lynx-eyed. Eyes like Lynceus. Eyes like an eagle.

An expression applied to people with abnormally good eyesight. The first two emerge from the Greeks, wherein a hero by the name of Lynceus was believed to have been able to see even through walls.

To split logs with a key and open doors with an axe.

Wisdom encapsulating the idea that we ought to use the right tools in the right situations. It is a waste of time and effort to use the wrong tools in any situation.

Two men can keep a secret if one of them is dead.

An adage referring to the problem of keeping secrets. It seems that men, in general, are very likely to blab about a secret at one time or another.

Conscience makes cowards of us all.

Expresses the age old problem that we often are unable to live up to the promptings of our conscience. It is often, if not always, because we fear persecution or humiliation that we disobey the compulsions of our conscience.

Spare the rod, spoil the child.

Parental wisdom noting that rotten, spoiled children are often the result of weak parenting techniques. There is a modern tendency against corporal punishment which has led to a less respectful and decent generation.

Fortune favors the brave.

Wisdom expressing the idea that the treasures of fortune are only won by those brave of enough to act. Cowards are often unable to act in the heat of the moment.

Procrastination is the thief of time.

The problem with procrastination is that it often wastes all of our time. We put off tomorrow what ought to be done today and only manage to spend all of our time idly.

A watched pot never boils.

Wisdom noting that watchfulness and attentiveness make it difficult for problems to arise.

He who drinks a little too much drinks too much.

An adage warning against the excuses people often make for their vices. When someone has a vice, they often try to limit censure by saying they do it only a "little too much." The fact is, though, that you are still doing something which ought not to be done at all.

Good Fences make Good Neighbors

The problem with neighbors is that they can often be difficult. This adage from the poet Robert Frost expresses the idea that limited contact with one's neighbors leads to neighborly relations. The adage is ironic, though, in that the no contact with one's neighbor is not really a neighborly relation.

A chain is only as strong as its weakest link.

An adage expressing the notion that the weakest member of a group defines the strength of that group. For instance, the 300 Spartans who defended Thermopylae from the Persian Empire was able to do so until one of their own betrayed them and told the Persians how they could rout the Spartan army.

A journey of a thousand miles begins with a single step.

Another adage referring to the fact that any every great work requires a beginning. If there is no beginning then there can be no end.

A leopard cannot change its spots.

Often used in a cynical context, this adage succinctly expresses the idea that certain things can never change. A leopard will always act like a leopard, just as a wicked man will always act wickedly.

A man with a hammer sees every problem as a nail.

Most people tend to solve problems using the approaches they are accustomed to using. A lawyer will look at the legal aspects of a problem whereas a craftsman will look at the logistics of getting something done.

A prophet is not recognized in his own land.

Refers to the troubling fact that great men are often rejected in the places where they are most familiar. The prophets of the Bible were almost unexclusively persecuted by the Jewish people. It can refer to anyone who attempts to warn their friends, family, or countrymen about impending disaster if they refuse to change their ways.

All roads lead to Rome.

This adage can be taken in several respects. In the days of the Roman Empire, this adage was meant to convey the truth that all roads would ultimately lead one to Rome since it was the capital of the most powerful empire of the age.

It can be applied metaphorically to cities and places today that possess a concentration of capital, power, and prestige. It can also be used in a spiritual sense as the city of Rome houses the Holy See; the meaning in this

Do not cast your pearls before swine.

A biblical adage warning those with talents and wisdom to refrain from wasting their efforts upon persons of low intelligence and ungraciousness.

Do not cry over spilt milk

A parable with a two-fold meaning: one should not cry over trivial matters nor over things which cannot be changed.

Fact is stranger than fiction.

Encapsulates the notion that what occurs in reality is often far stranger than any story one can make up. For instance, in one case a man hired a thug to throw acid in a woman's face. The man was imprisoned for his vile conduct for a period of more than ten years. When he was released he and the woman he physically scarred with acid married.

Fools rush in where angels fear to tread.

Refers to the problematic task of sorting out the truly brave from the foolish and reckless. This a problem addressed by Aristotle in his famous *Nicomachean Ethics*. There are two different vices attached to every virtue; one lies in excess, the other in deficiency. One who is lacking courage is called a coward. One who has a reasonable amount of courage is called brave. One who has an excessive amount of "courage" cannot be said to be courageous at all- rather he is reckless and foolish. If something as powerful as an angel is wary about something, only a fool would be rash enough to rush into it.

Imitation is the sincerest form of flattery.

Although many express their admirations for others with words and gestures, if they do not attempt to emulate the behavior of the people they claim to admire it can be said that they must no admire that person that much. Those who try to act like those they admire are truly giving credit to that person since they are trying to become like them in some way.

Mighty oaks from little acorns grow.

Great things often have small beginnings.

No man can serve two masters.

The problem with serving two masters occurs when inevitably the two masters order or desire contradictory things. The servant then has to choose to obey one master or the other.

Practice what you preach.

An injunction against hypocrisy. If those who teach others how to act fail to live up to their own standard, they reduce the credibility of their teachings.

Rome was not built in a day.

Great things require time and patience.

Slow and steady wins the race.

Those who go about their tasks carefully and slowly often finish faster than those who expend a great deal of energy unwisely.

Strike while the iron is hot.

An expression which advises us to act at the moment when a favorable outcome is most plausible. In order to craft a sword, one must strike the metal when it is hot- if it cools it becomes impossible to shape the sword. The same principle applies to decision making; one should execute tasks at the opportune moment since it may pass and never present itself again.

Take care of the pence, and the pounds will take care of themselves.

Take care of the small things like expenses and the profits will follow in a bigger fashion comparing monetary pounds to pence.

Talk is cheap.

Don't just talk about it. The effort and the doing is the key part. Don't just talk about helping others but jump in and do the work as well.

The best things in life are free.

Many become unfocused and fooled into thinking that the best things in life cost money. This is absolutely untrue as most of the greatest goods common to all men are free. The air we breathe and the sun which illuminates our world is available to all men without respect to class, gender, or age.

The early bird catches the worm.

Refers to the idea that beginning one's day early is a sure route to successful day and life. A comic reinterpretation of this adage is that "the early bird gets the worm, but the early worm gets eaten."

The grass is always greener on the other side of the fence.

This adage expresses a sentiment common to all men that the possessions or lifestyle of other people is greater than theirs, despite them not actually having any proof to support it.

The road to Hell is paved with good intentions.

Refers to the fact that many commit vile acts with good intentions.

The squeaking wheel gets the grease.

An adage which advises us that if we wish to get something accomplished we must be diligent and persistent about accomplishing it.

There is an exception to every rule.

Refers to the problem of crafting rules and regulations; there is always a loophole or situation that does not quite fit under the rules. Ambiguities and imperfect laws are the sole reason lawyers exist as their job is to apply imperfect rules to unique and unanticipated situations.

There are always more fish in the sea.

An adage often used in a romantic context. It is used to allay the disappointment or sorrow of someone who has been rejected by a girl or boy they were attracted to. It helps because it reminds the despondent lover that there are more girls out there.

There is no fool like an old fool.

There appears to be an almost universal hatred of elderly fools in world civilizations. This hatred is not unfounded or cruel, but in fact is very appropriate. An old fool is one who, despite living a long life, has not acquired any wisdom.

There is no smoke without fire.

An expression of the idea that some signs must necessarily point to another occurrence. Smoke always indicates the existence of fire.

Those who do not learn from history are doomed to repeat it.

A quote from the man of letters George Santayana. Those who do not learn lessons from unfortunate experience are most certainly going to experience the same misfortunes again.

Those who live in glass houses should not throw stones.

Those who, due to some weakness, lack the ability to defend themselves should not attack others who are capable of retaliating.

You can have too much of a good thing.

Refers to the problem of excess. When one has too much of a good thing it can become a bad thing. For instance, the gluttonous man is the man who eats too much food.

You can lead a horse to water, but you cannot make it drink.

One can lead others to certain conclusions, but it is up to them to believe those conclusions.

You cannot have your cake and eat it too.

An adage advising us that certain actions must necessarily preclude us from doing or having other things.

You cannot get blood out of a stone.

An adage admonishing fruitless or pointless activity.

You cannot make an omelette without breaking eggs.

An adage expressing the fact that to accomplish some things one has to give up other things. It is impossible to cook an omelette without eggs; it is impossible to go to law school and medical school at the same time. The adage advises us to make our decisions wisely since we preclude ourselves from another decision each time we make one.

Youth is wasted on the young.

An adage bewailing the fact that the young never listen to their elders who wish they would have lived their lives differently in youth.

Author Bio

Enrique Fiesta

I live in Southwest Florida and I enjoy studying the liberal arts, especially poetry and philosophy, attending Mass, and reading the classics. I studied Latin and Greek language and literature at university and I am currently pursuing a degree in law.

Check out some of the other JD-Biz Publishing books

Gardening Series on Amazon

Health Learning Series

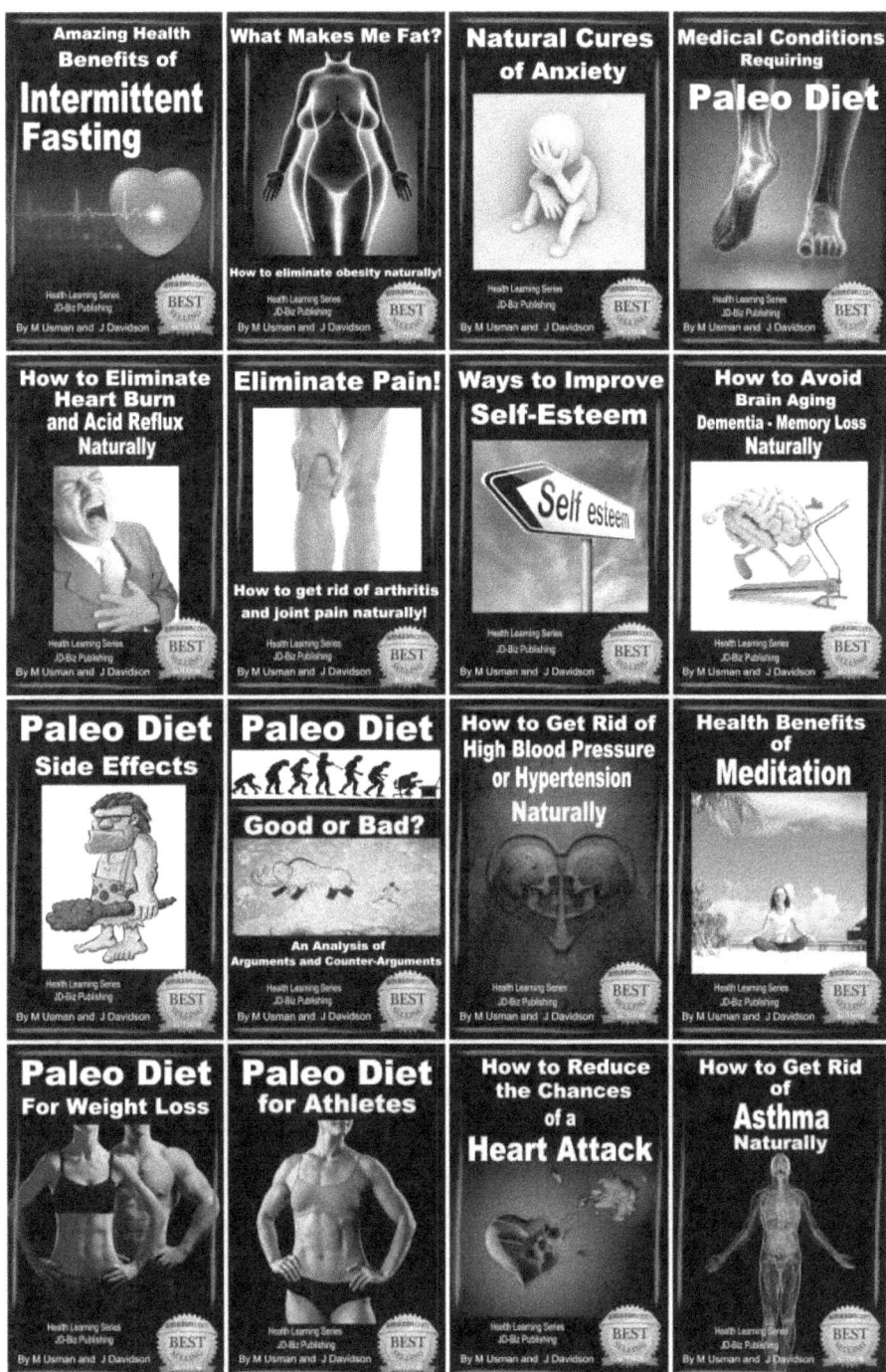

Learn To Draw Series

How to Build and Plan Books

Entrepreneur Book Series

Our books are available at

1. Amazon.com

2. Barnes and Noble

3. Itunes

4. Kobo

5. Smashwords

6. Google Play Books

Publisher

JD-Biz Corp

P O Box 374

Mendon, Utah 84325

http://www.jd-biz.com/